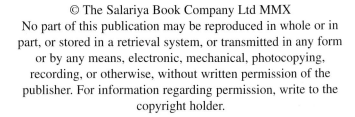

Author:
John Malam studied ancient history and archeology at the University of Birmingham, England, before working as an archeologist at the Ironbridge Gorge Museum in Shropshire. He is now an author, specializing in nonfiction books for children. He lives in Cheshire, England, with his wife and their two children. Find out more at: www.johnmalam.co.uk

Artist:
Mark Bergin was born in Hastings, England, in 1961. He studied at Eastbourne College of Art and specializes in historical reconstructions, aviation, and maritime subjects. He lives in Bexhill-on-Sea, England, with his wife and children.

Series creator:
David Salariya was born in Dundee, Scotland. He has illustrated a wide range of books and has created and designed many new series for publishers in the UK and overseas. David established The Salariya Book Company in 1989. He lives in Brighton, England, with his wife, illustrator Shirley Willis, and their son, Jonathan.

Editor:
Stephen Haynes

Editorial Assistants:
Mark Williams, Tanya Kant

© The Salariya Book Company Ltd MMX
No part of this publication may be reproduced in whole or in part, or stored in a retrieval system, or transmitted in any form or by any means, electronic, mechanical, photocopying, recording, or otherwise, without written permission of the publisher. For information regarding permission, write to the copyright holder.

Published in Great Britain in 2010 by
The Salariya Book Company Ltd
25 Marlborough Place, Brighton BN1 1UB

ISBN-13: 978-0-531-20474-0 (lib. bdg.)   978-0-531-13783-3 (pbk.)
ISBN-10: 0-531-20474-X (lib. bdg.)   0-531-13783-X (pbk.)
All rights reserved.
Published in 2010 in the United States
by Franklin Watts
An imprint of Scholastic Inc.
Published simultaneously in Canada.

A CIP catalog record for this book is available
from the Library of Congress.

Printed and bound in China.
Printed on paper from sustainable sources.
1 2 3 4 5 6 7 8 9 10 R 19 18 17 16 15 14 13 12 11 10

SCHOLASTIC, FRANKLIN WATTS, and associated logos are trademarks and/or registered trademarks of Scholastic Inc.

PAPER FROM
SUSTAINABLE
FORESTS

You Wouldn't Want to Be a Secret Agent During World War II!

Written by
John Malam

Illustrated by
Mark Bergin

Created and designed by
David Salariya

A Perilous Mission Behind Enemy Lines

Franklin Watts®
An Imprint of Scholastic Inc.
NEW YORK • TORONTO • LONDON • AUCKLAND • SYDNEY
MEXICO CITY • NEW DELHI • HONG KONG
DANBURY, CONNECTICUT

Contents

Introduction

France, your country, needs you! It's May 1940, and countries across Europe are fighting for survival in World War II. Denmark, the Netherlands, and Belgium have all surrendered to Nazi Germany, and now the German army has invaded France. French cities are falling to the invaders, and German troops are moving toward Paris, the French capital. As a wireless (radio) operator in the French army, your job is to send messages from your commanders to the troops. It will be a terrible day if France surrenders to Germany! What would you do then? Become a prisoner of war? Escape and become a refugee? Or could you find a way to carry on the fight?

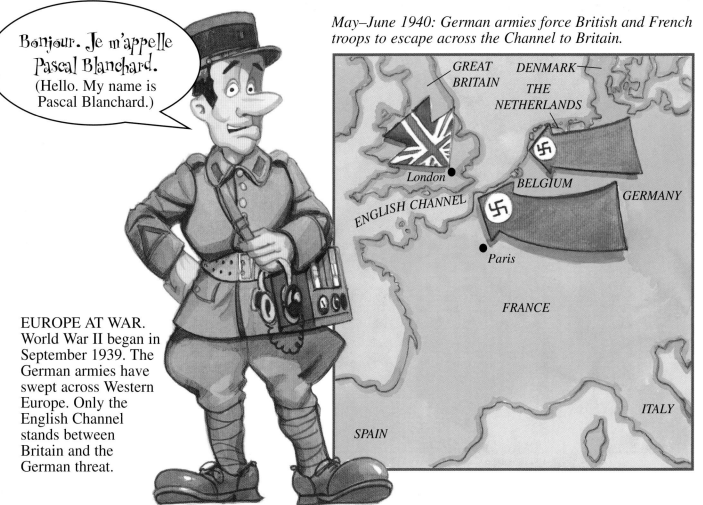

Bonjour. Je m'appelle Pascal Blanchard.
(Hello. My name is Pascal Blanchard.)

EUROPE AT WAR. World War II began in September 1939. The German armies have swept across Western Europe. Only the English Channel stands between Britain and the German threat.

May–June 1940: German armies force British and French troops to escape across the Channel to Britain.

GREAT BRITAIN
DENMARK
THE NETHERLANDS
London
BELGIUM
GERMANY
ENGLISH CHANNEL
Paris
FRANCE
ITALY
SPAIN

Refugee! Escape to Freedom

You will never forget Saturday, June 22, 1940. France surrendered to Germany, and you were ordered to send the bad news to French troops and tell them to lay down their weapons. For them, the war was over—France was beaten. But you vow to fight on. You will not surrender!

You flee to Britain, dressed as a civilian. You are one of thousands of refugees escaping from Nazi-occupied Europe—but the British have to make sure you are not a German secret agent trying to sneak into the country. You are taken to London, where members of MI5 (the secret British Security Service) check you out. They are interested in your language skills. Why?

What languages do you speak?

I think this one could be quite useful to us.

Countdown to War

1921: Adolf Hitler gains control of the Nazi Party in Germany. By 1932, the Nazis are Germany's most popular political party.

1933. Hitler becomes chancellor—leader of the German government. He plans to build a German empire that will last for 1,000 years.

1936. Hitler sends troops into the Rhineland—which Germany had been forbidden to do since the end of World War I.

1938. Germany seizes Austria and part of Czechoslovakia.

SEPTEMBER 1, 1939. Germany invades Poland. Britain and France declare war on Germany on September 3.

JUNE 23, 1940. The day after France surrenders, Hitler flies to Paris and tours the French capital.

The words of British Prime Minister Neville Chamberlain, broadcast September 3, 1939.

Interviewed! But What's the Job?

La France ou la Grande Bretagne?
(France or Britain?)

It feels safe in Britain at first. But when German bombs fall on central London during the night of August 23, 1940, you know the war is getting closer—and you want to have a part in it.

You don't have long to wait! You are asked to attend an interview at the Northumberland Hotel in London. An officer from the British army asks you lots of questions about France, about yourself, and about your work as a wireless operator. Sometimes he speaks in English, sometimes in French. It seems as though he's testing you, but he doesn't give you any clue about what he's looking for.

WHICH SIDE ARE YOU ON? Only one of your parents is French—the other is British. This means you have dual nationality and can serve in either the British or the French armed forces. The choice is yours.

FREE FRENCH FORCES. If both your parents were French, you would have had no choice but to join the Free French Forces, who have continued the fight against Germany.

GENERAL CHARLES DE GAULLE. A leading member of the French government, de Gaulle (right) was in London when France surrendered to Germany. He has made London his base and has called for French soldiers to join the Free French Forces.

Cross of Lorraine

The Cross of Lorraine is the symbol of the Free French.

9

You're Picked! Now Set Europe Ablaze!

Xou are called back for a second and then a third interview, and both are as puzzling as the first. You don't find out what they have in mind until the end of the third interview. The British want you to become an agent in Section F (the France section) of the Special Operations Executive (SOE). It's a top-secret military group whose mission is to cause maximum disruption to the Germans. In the words of Prime Minister Winston Churchill, your job is to "set Europe ablaze." It sounds exciting—and dangerous!

Welcome, Second Lieutenant Blanchard. Your codename is Léon.*

Yes, sir! Thank you, sir!

WINSTON CHURCHILL (right) became prime minister of Britain on May 10, 1940. He gave Dr. Hugh Dalton, the minister of economic warfare, the job of setting up the Special Operations Executive. Its headquarters are on Baker Street in London.

*Léon means "lion." It's a popular name in France.

Today, July 22, 1940, the War Cabinet has agreed to set up the SOE.

Your New Job

SECRET MISSION. You'll be trained to work as an SOE agent and then sent on a dangerous mission to France. You'll either be sneaked into occupied France by fishing boat (let's hope you don't get seasick), or dropped in by parachute.

Handy Hint

Before you go on your first mission, write your will. There's a good chance you won't survive.

WIRELESS. Once you're in France, you will use your skills as a wireless operator to send and receive secret messages by Morse code. Don't let the Germans catch you!

·_·· · ·_
__·_· · ·__· ·_·· ·_· __·_·*

*Morse code for "Léon calling."

CAPTURED. If the Germans arrest you, you can expect to be interrogated—even tortured—until you reveal your secrets.

WAAFs. The SOE isn't just for men. Women are also recruited, and they join the Women's Auxiliary Air Force.

EXECUTED. If the Germans decide you are a spy (which is one way of describing you), you might be executed by a firing squad.

11

The Right Stuff? School for Danger*

Y ou are now considered a student, and you are put through a training program to find out whether you have what it takes to be a secret agent. You are tested by psychologists, psychiatrists, and military trainers. If you fail the tests, you'll be sent home. But you pass—congratulations!

After you pass the tests, you're sent to a paramilitary school in northern Scotland, where you are given lessons in physical exercise, fieldcraft, sabotage skills, weapons use, and silent killing. There are several of these schools in the Arisaig and Morar areas of Inverness-shire. The countryside there is isolated and rugged.

1. THE SHAKE

It's so good to see you!

Getting in Shape

RUNNING. You are sent on long runs in bad weather while wearing all your combat gear. This builds up your strength and stamina.

OBSTACLE COURSE AND TUMBLING. You walk along a narrow wooden beam and practice forward rolls. This sharpens your reflexes and improves your balance.

ROPEWORK. You climb ropes and crawl across rope nets. This improves your agility.

*School for Danger *is the title of a movie about the SOE made in 1947.*

2. THE TWIST

3. THE KILL

Er... what are you doing?

OK—you can stop now, sir!

Handy Hint

Stay away from the bar! If you get drunk, the SOE will know that you can't be trusted with secrets.

COMBAT TRAINING. An instructor teaches you the technique of silent killing.
1. He shakes your hand.
2. Then he twists you around.
3. He pulls a dagger and pretends to stab you.

Learning New Skills

PLASTIC EXPLOSIVE. You are taught how to handle plastic explosive and how to use it to make bombs.

Why me?

SURVIVING IN THE WILD. You practice living off the land— finding food, making fires, and building shelters.

MAP, COMPASS, DAGGER. You learn to read maps, use a compass, and handle the SOE's double-edged dagger.

Parachuted! Earning Your Wings

As part of your military training, you are taught to parachute from an airplane. This is because your secret mission might begin with a drop into Nazi-occupied France. You make several jumps, including one at night. Take a deep breath, hold tight, jump!

The training is at No.1 Parachute Training School, at the Royal Air Force (RAF) base at Ringway in Cheshire, just south of the city of Manchester. Not every student passes the parachute training and earns the Parachutist Badge.

BALLOON JUMP. You make your first jump at RAF Ringway from a box attached to a barrage balloon. It's only 700 feet (213 meters) above the ground—but it feels much higher!

Aaaargh!

SWINGING. You start by swinging from a roof beam. That gets you used to being off the ground.

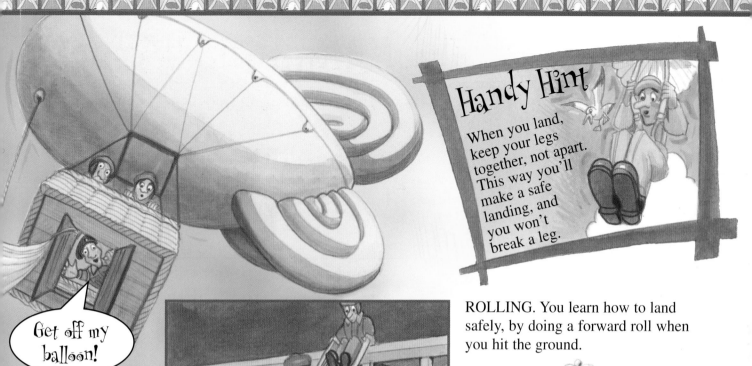

Handy Hint

When you land, keep your legs together, not apart. This way you'll make a safe landing, and you won't break a leg.

Get off my balloon!

ROLLING. You learn how to land safely, by doing a forward roll when you hit the ground.

WINGS. You earn the Parachutist Badge—your "wings"—for successfully completing the training.

REAL JUMP 1. You make your first jump at night, out of a Handley Page Halifax, one of the RAF's heavy bomber planes. You jump from a height of about 4,000 feet (1,220 meters).

REAL JUMP 2. Your next jump is in daytime. You jump with a leg bag dangling beneath you. This is how you'll carry your equipment into France.

No More School! Training Is Over

More New Skills

LOCK-PICKING. You learn how to open locks without a key. This will be useful for breaking into places—and for getting out of handcuffs!

SECRET MEETINGS. You learn how to meet your contacts without the enemy suspecting a thing.

The last part of your training is at Beaulieu ("BEW-lee"), a grand country estate in Hampshire, in the south of Britain. For the next three weeks, the SOE teaches you how to survive behind enemy lines. The worst part of the course is the mock interrogation. You're dragged from your bed in the middle of the night, tied to a chair, and bombarded with questions by a trainer pretending to be a Nazi officer. It's meant to scare you, and it does. Whatever happens, don't give away any secrets, or you'll fail the course!

DEAD DROP. You learn how to hide messages in safe places where the enemy will not find them.

MORSE CODE. You're taught how to send and receive messages without being caught. Keep messages short, and send them from different places.

CHECKING OUT A TARGET. You learn how to identify a good target, such as an ammunitions factory, and then figure out how to sneak inside.

SABOTAGE. You are taught ways to damage the enemy's equipment so it can't be used again.

Warum sind sie hier, englischer Spion?
(Why are you here, English spy?)

I... must... not... tell him!

Grrrr!

Handy Hint

If you are arrested by the Germans, keep your mouth shut for as long as possible. This will give other agents time to escape.

If You Fail

SENT AWAY. If you fail the final stage of the training, you will be a problem. You know too much—including the identities of the other students. It will be too risky to send you back to your real life. Instead, you will be sent to a remote part of Scotland, far away from the nearest town. You'll stay there until everything that you know is out of date and of no use to the enemy.

Goodies! Your Bag of Tricks

As a fully trained SOE agent, you have access to an amazing range of special devices to use on missions. Every one of these top-secret tools is designed to do a specific job.

To disguise your appearance, wear false teeth and rub wrinkling cream onto your skin—this will make you look older than you really are.

Get used to working with harmless-looking objects that are really booby traps. The SOE has experts to teach you how and when to use them. Practice firing a sleeve gun at a target—it looks just like a metal tube, but it packs a deadly shot. It just might save your life!

S-PHONE. A wireless device for communicating by speech (not Morse code) with a plane or boat.

BICYCLE GENERATOR. Keep pedaling. This will charge the batteries of your wireless device.

Learning to use a sleeve gun

FIREPOT. A metal case packed with thermite and gunpowder. It burns with an intense heat and sets fire to whatever is nearby.

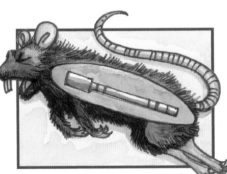

EXPLOSIVE RAT. This dead rat is packed with plastic explosive. It explodes when thrown onto a fire.

INCENDIARY SUITCASE. A booby-trapped suitcase that bursts into flames when opened. Leave it for the enemy to find!

18

He won't know what hit him!

BANG!

But remember, you can only use it once.

Handy Hint

You can hide a bulky wireless device inside a bundle of sticks. It's the best way to camouflage it.

FAKE LOGS AND FRUIT. Hollowed-out logs, fruits, and vegetables made from plaster or papier-mâché can be used to hide ammunition and other small items.

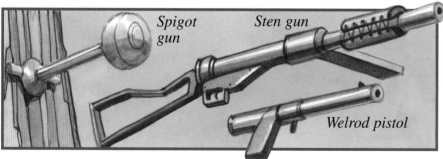

Spigot gun

Sten gun

Welrod pistol

SPIGOT GUN. When a passerby accidentally touches a wire attached to this booby trap, it fires a single bullet at him.

NOISELESS GUNS. The Sten gun has a range of 225 feet (69 meters). The Welrod pistol can strike from about 24 feet (7.3 meters).

TRIPWIRE AND MATCHES. Steel tripwire is used to set booby traps. Slow-burning matches are for lighting fuses for explosives.

Jump! You're Dropped into France

Now that your training is over, you are sent to an airbase in the east of Britain. Your first mission will be an "in and out" mission to France. You and two other agents are going to sabotage a factory that makes tires for German trucks. The factory was bombed—but not destroyed—by the RAF. Now your team is going to wreck it for good.

You're dropped into France at night, by a Whitley bomber that flies in low to avoid enemy radar. At the drop zone, you meet a group of fighters from the French Resistance. They've been expecting you and will help you on the mission.

The Sabotage Team

TEAM LEADER. He's an experienced SOE agent who has survived several missions in Nazi-occupied France. Obey him.

WIRELESS OPERATOR. This is you. It's your job to keep in contact with headquarters in Britain. You are the team's ears.

EXPLOSIVES EXPERT. Plastic explosive, gelignite, grenades, incendiary devices, time switches, and fuses are in this man's hands.

This time it's for real!

Handy Hint

If you think you might get airsick, take some airsickness pills before you leave.

Blecch! I should've taken some airsickness pills!

RESISTANCE FIGHTERS. These are French men and women who fight against the Nazis in France. They're on your side.

EQUIPMENT. Apart from the equipment you carry with you, everything you need is inside containers that were parachuted with you. Don't lose them!

Blend In! Be a Good Actor

The Resistance fighters collect your team's equipment, gather the parachutes, and rush you away from the drop zone. Nothing is left behind, so the Germans won't suspect anything. It's too risky to keep the team together, so the Resistance takes each of you to a different hideout. You go to a farm, where a French woman pretends to be your wife. You wear French clothes, speak French, and do nothing to attract the Germans' attention. After a few days of blending in, you cycle past the tire factory. It looks like you're on an ordinary bike ride, but you're really checking out the target. There's a scary moment when German soldiers ask to see your identity papers. The papers are fake, but you hope they're good enough to fool the enemy.

FAKE FARMER. You work as if you are a farmer. But all the while, you're waiting for word from the team leader about when to attack the factory.

Checking Out the Target

GUARDS. German soldiers guard the factory gates and patrol the perimeter fence. It's very well guarded.

ARMAMENTS. There are guns all around the factory. Some are for firing at airplanes. Others are designed to shoot intruders.

WEAK POINT. You search for a weakness in the fence. It will be your way to get into the factory.

Handy Hint

Don't write down anything that could be used as evidence against you. Commit everything to memory.

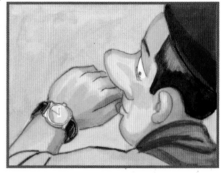

TIMETABLE. When you enter the factory, everything will have to be timed to the second. Figure out exactly how long each stage of the attack will take.

TIRES. Finished tires are stored next to rail lines. You must destroy the tires before they're loaded on the trains.

23

Kaboom! Hit the Target

On mission day, your sabotage team comes together, and the team leader carefully goes over your timetable. You check and double-check your wireless device. The minutes slowly tick away, and no one speaks. You are as nervous as the others, but you try not to show it. At last it's time to go. You wait until the perimeter guards are out of sight, and then dash to the fence and crawl under it. The team splits up. The explosive expert sets his bombs among the finished tires while you sneak inside the factory to sabotage the machinery. The bombs explode, and their dull thuds are followed by orange fireballs. Sirens wail, and searchlights flash across the ground. The job's done. It's time to leave!

Mehr Wasser!
(More water!)

,⌐, .. ⁻‾ ⁻‾ .. ⁻. ⁻⁻
.‾ ⁻⁻⁻ ....⁻ ....⁻ .....*

Mission Timetable

18:00 HOURS.** You send a coded wireless message from "Léon" to Britain, asking for a pick-up plane to come at 03:45 hours.

20:00 HOURS. Check all the explosives. Set their fuses and time switches so they'll be ready to explode.

23:45 HOURS. Put camouflage paint on your face. This will make it harder for the Germans to see you in the dark.

*"Pick up at 03:45."   **6:00 p.m., using the 24-hour clock. It's pronounced "eighteen hundred hours."

03:00 HOURS.
Mission accomplished!

Handy Hint

Put the explosives on the same parts of each machine. That way the Germans can't use parts from one machine to repair another.

01:30 HOURS. Enter the factory through the weak point that you found in the perimeter fence.

01:45 HOURS. Once you're inside the factory, place the explosive charges among the machines.

02:30 HOURS. Leave the factory. Will you make it to the pick-up zone in time to catch the rescue plane?

Safe House! You're on the Run

Within minutes of the explosions, the night sky is lit up with searchlights. The pilot of the pick-up plane decides that it's too dangerous to land, and he turns around. You're stranded!

All around you are the shouts of German search parties and the barks of their dogs. The Resistance fighters take you to a safe house, where you can stay until a new pick up can be arranged.

SPLIT UP. Each agent is taken to a different safe house. This way there is less chance of everyone in the team being caught.

ON THE MOVE. You can't stay in the same safe house for too long, so the Resistance fighters move you around. You get used to being carted from place to place.

IN DANGER. The men and women of the French Resistance risk their lives to protect you. If they are caught sheltering you, they will be severely punished, and may be put to death.

27

Picked Up! It's Time to Leave

Get a move on!

After a few days, the German search parties and their dogs are called off. You send a wireless message to Britain and wait for the reply. It says a plane will be sent tonight!

When darkness falls, the Resistance fighters take you to a field, where you join your comrades. The Resistance fighters place two rows of burning torches on the ground to mark out a temporary airstrip. Suddenly, a tiny RAF Lysander plane drops from the sky and heads for the field. It will touch down and take off again in less than two minutes, so get ready to run up to it and climb on board. The pilot will soon have you back in Britain—but it won't be long before you return to France on another daring mission!

Getting You Home

KEEP IT SECRET. The fewer people who know about the pick up, the better. The pilot won't land if he thinks there's a problem.

ALL ABOARD. The Lysander carries three or four passengers at most. It's a squeeze, but you've got to get in.

GET READY. The team leader gives the OK to the pilot, who takes off as fast as he can. The Resistance fighters wave good-bye.

Handy Hint

Stand by the *left* line of the airstrip lights. The pilot has orders to shoot people who stand in the wrong place— even you!

FLYING HIGH. The pilot flies high to avoid flak from the German anti-aircraft guns on the ground. It's a bumpy flight.

WELL DONE! You are congratulated on the success of the mission. But there's no time to relax, as you'll soon be sent on another. Good luck!

Au revoir et bonne chance. (Good-bye and good luck.)

Bon voyage! (Have a safe journey!)

29

Glossary

Airstrip A runway on which planes take off and land.

Anti-aircraft gun A large gun that is designed to shoot down airplanes from the ground.

Barrage balloon A huge balloon tied to the ground by cables. The cables act as an obstacle to enemy bomber planes.

Booby trap A hidden bomb or weapon that goes off when the enemy stumbles upon it.

Camouflage To hide objects or people by coloring them so they blend into the background.

Chancellor The title of the person who leads Germany's government.

Civilian A person who is not a member of the armed forces.

Dead drop A hiding place where secret agents leave messages.

Drop zone The area into which parachutists are dropped.

Fieldcraft Outdoor skills such as survival techniques and map-reading.

Flak Gunfire from anti-aircraft guns.

Free French Forces An organization of French men and women who continued to fight against Germany after France surrendered in 1940.

Fuse A device, usually connected to a timer, that causes a bomb to explode.

Incendiary Describing something that can cause a fire.

Interrogate To formally question a person.

Leg bag A bag of equipment tied to a parachutist's leg.

MI5 Stands for "Military Intelligence, Section 5." This security agency searches for enemy spies working inside Great Britain.

Morse code An alphabet of dots and dashes that was used to send messages across long distances.

Nazi A member of the National Socialist German Workers' Party (the Nazi Party), which ruled Germany from 1933 to 1945.

Occupied Invaded and ruled by an enemy country.

Paramilitary Describing military training for civilians rather than for members of the armed forces.

Perimeter The border of an area of land.

Psychiatrist A medical doctor who studies the human mind and treats patients with counseling and/or medicines.

Psychologist An expert in the human mind who treats patients with counseling.

Radar A system that uses radio waves to find moving objects in the sky, especially aircraft.

RAF Great Britain's Royal Air Force.

Refugee A person who leaves his or her own country to seek safety in another.

Resistance The small groups of French men and women who secretly fought the German forces that occupied France during World War II.

Sabotage The deliberate destruction of the enemy's equipment.

Safe house A building where it is safe for a wanted or hunted person to hide.

Special Operations Executive (SOE) A British government organization that was created in 1940 to spy on the Germans and sabotage their equipment.

Thermite A powder that burns at a very high temperature when lit.

Will A legal document giving instructions for dealing with a person's possessions after his or her death.

Wireless An old-fashioned word for "radio."

Index